The Life and Ministry of
JESUS CHRIST
The Cross and Resurrection

I0338182

*A NavPress resource published in alliance
with Tyndale House Publishers, Inc.*

NavPress is the publishing ministry of The Navigators, an international Christian organization and leader in personal spiritual development. NavPress is committed to helping people grow spiritually and enjoy lives of meaning and hope through personal and group resources that are biblically rooted, culturally relevant, and highly practical.

For more information, visit www.NavPress.com.

The Cross and the Resurrection LMJC

© 1996 by The Navigators. All rights reserved.

A NavPress resource published in alliance with Tyndale House Publishers, Inc.

NAVPRESS and the NAVPRESS logo are registered trademarks of NavPress, The Navigators, Colorado Springs, CO. *TYNDALE* is a registered trademark of Tyndale House Publishers, Inc. Absence of ® in connection with marks of NavPress or other parties does not indicate an absence of registration of those marks.

ISBN 978-0-89109-971-0

Map: GeoSystems Global Corporation

This series was produced for NavPress with the assistance of The Livingstone Corporation. James C. Galvin, Valerie Weidemann, and Daryl J. Lucas, project editors.

All Scripture quotations, unless otherwise indicated, are taken from the Holy Bible, *New International Version*,® *NIV*.® Copyright © 1973, 1978, 1984, 2011 by Biblica, Inc.® Used by permission. All rights reserved worldwide.

CONTENTS

INTRODUCTION   5

LESSON ONE   FICKLE OR FAITHFUL?   9
Jesus teaches about the Holy Spirit and prayer (John 16:5-33)
Jesus prays for Himself and believers (John 17:1-26)
Jesus agonizes in the garden (Matthew 26:36-46)
Jesus is betrayed and arrested (John 18:2-11)

LESSON TWO   PRESUMED GUILTY   23
Jesus is questioned and condemned (Matthew 26:57, 59-68; 27:1)
Peter denies knowing Jesus (Mark 14:54,66-72)
Judas kills himself (Matthew 27:3-10)
Jesus stands trial before Pilate and Herod (John 18:28–19:16)

LESSON THREE   THE FINAL STEP   35
Jesus is crucified (Luke 23:26-49)
Jesus is buried (John 19:38-42)
Jesus rises from the dead and appears to the women (Mark 16:1-11)

LESSON FOUR   WE MEET AGAIN   45
Jesus appears to two believers traveling on the road (Luke 24:13-35)
Jesus appears to the disciples behind locked doors (Luke 24:36-43)
Jesus appears to the disciples including Thomas (John 20:24-31)
Jesus appears to the disciples while fishing (John 21:1-25)

LESSON FIVE   SPREAD THE WORD!   57
Jesus gives the Great Commission (Matthew 28:16-20)
Jesus appears to the disciples in Jerusalem (Luke 24:44-49)
Jesus ascends into heaven (Mark 16:19-20)

HARMONY OF THE LIFE AND MINISTRY OF JESUS CHRIST   65

Study guides in the
LIFE AND MINISTRY OF JESUS CHRIST series:

The Beginning
Challenging Tradition
The Messiah
Following Jesus
Answering the Call
Final Teachings
The Cross and Resurrection

INTRODUCTION

If you want to learn more about Jesus Christ and become more like Him, then THE LIFE AND MINISTRY OF JESUS CHRIST series is for you and your small group. This seven-book Bible study spans all four Gospels, covers the entire life of Christ in chronological order, and emphasizes personal application of biblical truth. By using an inductive study format, THE LIFE AND MINISTRY OF JESUS CHRIST helps you investigate for yourself what Jesus did and what He taught.

Each guide has five lessons and may be studied in five sessions, or in as many as ten to twelve sessions if your group prefers a slower pace. For best results, each group member should study the passages listed and write out the answers to the questions — including the application questions in the side columns. Then, as you meet with your Bible study group or class you can discuss what you have observed and applied. Use the side columns to write out any additional insights or applications that emerge from the discussion. The emphasis on application helps to maintain a balance between factual knowledge and character development. The more time and prayer you invest in the study, the more you will gain from it.

In each section of a given lesson, one biblical passage will be the main focus of study. That passage is printed out for you. Additional passages may also be listed. Read them as you have time.

A separate leader's resource guide is available for THE LIFE AND MINISTRY OF JESUS CHRIST series that provides additional background for each lesson and optional discussion questions for the group.

The Scripture passages were arranged based on the order presented by A. T. Robertson in *A Harmony of the Gospels* (Harper & Brothers, 1950). A harmony is a sequencing of the four Gospel accounts of the life of Jesus in parallel form to facilitate a study of His life and ministry. You can find the harmony used in this study in the "Harmony of the Life and Ministry of Jesus Christ" in the back of each study guide.

A harmony shows the events in the life of Christ in chronological order. Some events, such as the feeding of the five thousand, are recorded in all four Gospels; others, such as Jesus' interview with Nicodemus in the Gospel of John, appear in only one. Mark's Gospel is the most chronological; Matthew's follows themes more closely than chronology.

Without careful study and the aid of a harmony, the Gospels may appear to contain chronological discrepancies. The order of the material in each Gospel differs because Jesus taught the same truths, told the same parables, and performed similar miracles many times in His three-and-a-half year ministry. So Matthew recorded the contents of the Sermon on the Mount in one large section toward the beginning of Jesus' ministry (Matthew 5–7), while Luke wrote down similar teachings of Jesus throughout His ministry (Luke 6:17-49, 11:1-13, 13:22-30). Undoubtedly Jesus pronounced judgment on those who opposed and harassed Him a number of times, so Matthew tells of an incident in Galilee toward the middle of His ministry (Matthew 12:22-45) while Luke records another such confrontation, this time in Judea, later in His ministry (Luke 11:14-36). These are not contradictions but records of similar events.

This Bible study resulted from the diligent work of many men and women around the world. A team of Navigator staff realized the need for this study and began putting it together. Others field tested the material and made refinements. Still others read it and offered valuable advice. Then skilled editors shaped the study to its final form.

To all who have prayed and labored diligently, a hearty word of thanks. It is, in every sense, the result of a team effort, coached and coordinated by the Holy Spirit. As the Author of the Word of God, as Teacher and Interpreter of the Word to believers, and as the Divine Distributor of His gifts to them, the Holy Spirit has in a unique way directed the production of this study. His desire for its effectiveness must stem from His special ministry of revealing and glorifying Jesus Christ in our lives. To this purpose the study is dedicated.

> *"I have much more to say to you, more than you can now bear. But when he, the Spirit of truth, comes, he will guide you into all truth. He will not speak on his own; he will speak only what he hears, and he will tell you what is yet to come. He will bring glory to me by taking from what is mine and making it known to you. All that belongs to the Father is mine. That is why I said the Spirit will take from what is mine and make it known to you." (John 16:12-15)*

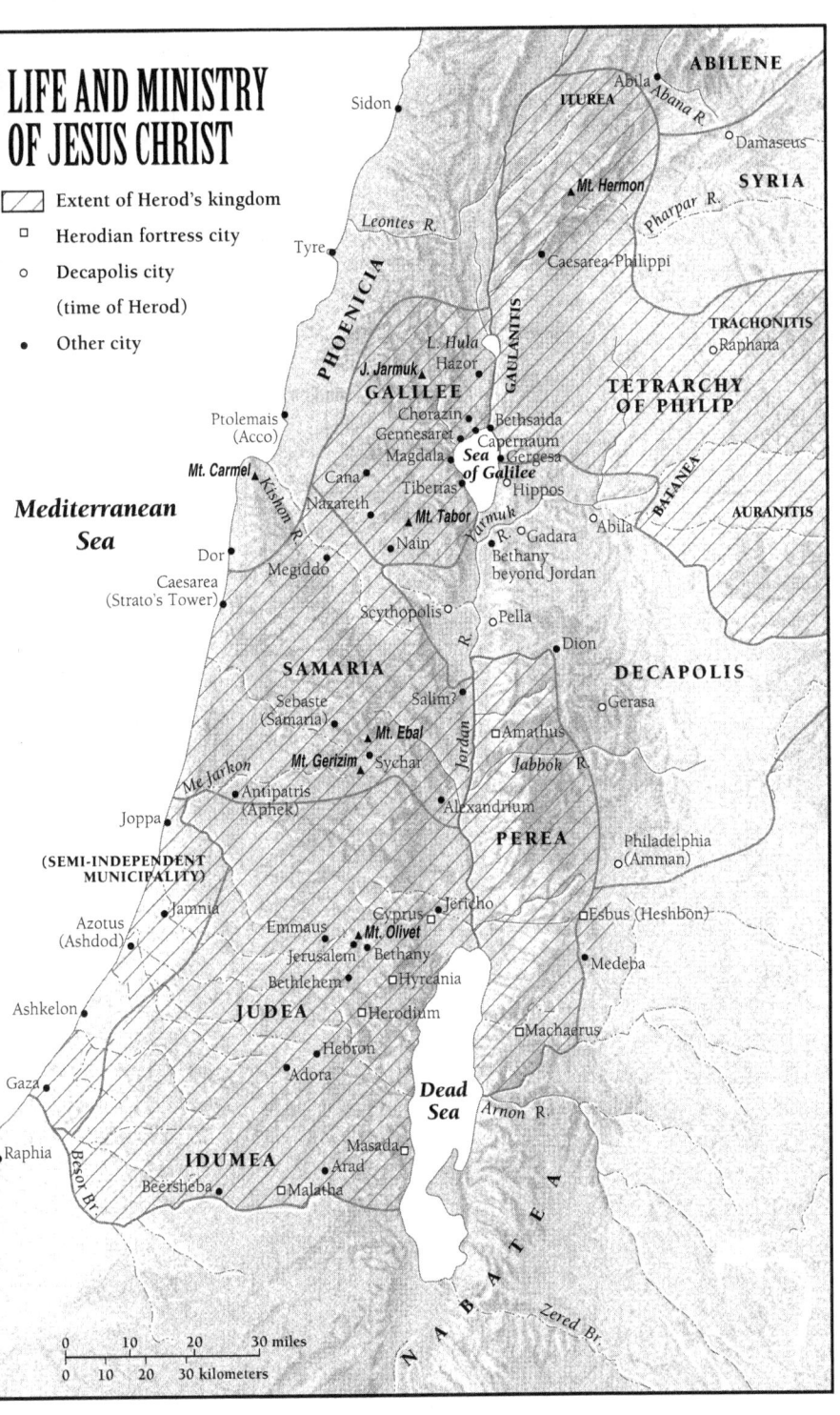

LESSON ONE
FICKLE OR FAITHFUL?

Some Christians have been forced to choose to renounce their faith or die for it! In this lesson, we'll see that the disciples faced the prospect of arrest, imprisonment, and death because of their faith in Christ. Although Jesus didn't give them the exact details of what would happen, He did tell them how to remain faithful in the midst of persecution and suffering. As we study Christ's words of warning and encouragement to them, we'll be challenged to recognize how our faith is tested and how to stay loyal to Christ.

JESUS TEACHES ABOUT THE HOLY SPIRIT AND PRAYER *John 16:5-33*

⁵"Now I am going to him who sent me, yet none of you asks me, 'Where are you going?' ⁶Because I have said these things, you are filled with grief. ⁷But I tell you the truth: It is for your good that I am going away. Unless I go away, the Counselor will not come to you; but if I go, I will send him to you. ⁸When he comes, he will convict the world of guilt in regard to sin and righteousness and judgment: ⁹in regard to sin, because men do not believe in me; ¹⁰in regard to righteousness, because I am going to the Father, where you can see me no longer; ¹¹and in regard to judgment, because the

Surely he took up our infirmities and carried our sorrows, yet we considered him stricken by God, smitten by him, and afflicted. But he was pierced for our transgressions, he was crushed for our iniquities; the punishment that brought us peace was upon him, and by his wounds we are healed.
(Isaiah 53:4-5)

prince of this world now stands condemned.

¹²"I have much more to say to you, more than you can now bear. ¹³But when he, the Spirit of truth, comes, he will guide you into all truth. He will not speak on his own; he will speak only what he hears, and he will tell you what is yet to come. ¹⁴He will bring glory to me by taking from what is mine and making it known to you. ¹⁵All that belongs to the Father is mine. That is why I said the Spirit will take from what is mine and make it known to you.

¹⁶"In a little while you will see me no more, and then after a little while you will see me."

¹⁷Some of his disciples said to one another, "What does he mean by saying, 'In a little while you will see me no more, and then after a little while you will see me,' and 'Because I am going to the Father'?" ¹⁸They kept asking, "What does he mean by 'a little while'? We don't understand what he is saying."

¹⁹Jesus saw that they wanted to ask him about this, so he said to them, "Are you asking one another what I meant when I said, 'In a little while you will see me no more, and then after a little while you will see me'? ²⁰I tell you the truth, you will weep and mourn while the world rejoices. You will grieve, but your grief will turn to joy. ²¹A woman giving birth to a child has pain because her time has come; but when her baby is born she forgets the anguish because of her joy that a child is born into the world. ²²So with you: Now is your time of grief, but I will see you again and you will rejoice, and no one will take away your joy. ²³In that day you will no longer ask me anything. I tell you the truth, my Father will give you whatever you ask in my name. ²⁴Until now you have not asked for anything in my name. Ask and you will receive, and your joy will be complete.

²⁵"Though I have been speaking figuratively, a time is coming when I will no longer use this kind of language but will tell you plainly about my Father. ²⁶In that day you will ask in my name. I am

not saying that I will ask the Father on your behalf. ²⁷*No, the Father himself loves you because you have loved me and have believed that I came from God.* ²⁸*I came from the Father and entered the world; now I am leaving the world and going back to the Father."*

²⁹*Then Jesus' disciples said, "Now you are speaking clearly and without figures of speech.* ³⁰*Now we can see that you know all things and that you do not even need to have anyone ask you questions. This makes us believe that you came from God."*

³¹*"You believe at last!" Jesus answered.* ³²*"But a time is coming, and has come, when you will be scattered, each to his own home. You will leave me all alone. Yet I am not alone, for my Father is with me.*

³³*"I have told you these things, so that in me you may have peace. In this world you will have trouble. But take heart! I have overcome the world."* (John 16:5-33)

Just a few hours before His death, Jesus stopped using figurative language and told His disciples plainly why He had to leave them. The disciples, who had been desperately trying to understand what Jesus was saying, were finally convinced that He knew everything that would happen because He was from God. Jesus told them that despite the struggles they would inevitably face, they could find peace in Him. In the same way, we can claim the peace of Jesus in the worst circumstances.

1. How did Jesus explain to His disciples His coming death and the benefits it would bring them?

2. According to Jesus, what role does the Holy Spirit play in the world and the lives of believers?

What trouble or problem are you facing right now?

3. What struggles are inevitable in the Christian life?

How can you depend on the Holy Spirit to guide you?

4. How do Jesus' words in this passage encourage you?

JESUS PRAYS FOR HIMSELF AND BELIEVERS *John 17:1-26*

¹*After Jesus said this, he looked toward heaven and prayed:*

"Father, the time has come. Glorify your Son, that your Son may glorify you. ²For you granted him authority over all people that he might give eternal life to all those you have given him. ³Now this is eternal life: that they may know you, the only true God, and Jesus Christ, whom you have sent. ⁴I have brought you glory on earth by completing the work you gave me to do. ⁵And now, Father, glorify me in your presence with the glory I had with you before the world began.

⁶"I have revealed you to those whom you gave me out of the world. They were yours; you gave them to me and they have obeyed your word. ⁷Now they know that everything you have given me comes from you. ⁸For I gave them the words you gave me and they accepted them. They knew with certainty that I came from you, and they believed that you sent me. ⁹I pray for them. I am not praying for the world, but for those you have given me, for they are yours. ¹⁰All I have is yours, and all you have is mine. And glory has come to me through them.
¹¹I will remain in the world no longer, but they are still in the world, and I am coming to you. Holy Father, protect them by the power of your name—the name you gave me—so that they may be one as we are one. ¹²While I was with them, I protected them and kept them safe by that name you gave me. None has been lost except the one doomed to destruction so that Scripture would be fulfilled.

¹³"I am coming to you now, but I say these things while I am still in the world, so that they may have the full measure of my joy within them. ¹⁴I have given them your word and the world has hated them, for they are not of the world any more than I am of the world. ¹⁵My prayer is not that you take them out of the world but that you protect

them from the evil one. [16]They are not of the world, even as I am not of it. [17]Sanctify them by the truth; your word is truth. [18]As you sent me into the world, I have sent them into the world. [19]For them I sanctify myself, that they too may be truly sanctified.

[20]"My prayer is not for them alone. I pray also for those who will believe in me through their message, [21]that all of them may be one, Father, just as you are in me and I am in you. May they also be in us so that the world may believe that you have sent me. [22]I have given them the glory that you gave me, that they may be one as we are one: [23]I in them and you in me. May they be brought to complete unity to let the world know that you sent me and have loved them even as you have loved me.

[24]"Father, I want those you have given me to be with me where I am, and to see my glory, the glory you have given me because you loved me before the creation of the world.

[25]"Righteous Father, though the world does not know you, I know you, and they know that you have sent me. [26]I have made you known to them, and will continue to make you known in order that the love you have for me may be in them and that I myself may be in them." (John 17:1-26)

Jesus prayed out loud for the benefit of His disciples and all future believers. In His prayer, we learn that we are engaged in a great battle with the spiritual enemy until Jesus returns. But because we know that Jesus has overcome the world, we can live confidently and rely on His strength to help us remain true until the end. The key to experiencing joy in the midst of spiritual warfare is to live in intimate communion with Christ, the source of true joy.

5. Why does the world hate Jesus' followers?

6. How is it possible for us to be joyful even when we suffer?

7. How does the truth of God's Word sanctify us (that is, make us holy)?

What steps can you take today to strengthen your relationship with another believer?

8. For what reason does Jesus want believers to be unified?

How can you pursue more of Christ's joy and peace this week?

9. How can we promote unity?

JESUS AGONIZES IN THE GARDEN
Matthew 26:36-46, Mark 14:32-42, Luke 22:39-46, John 18:1

³⁶Then Jesus went with his disciples to a place called Gethsemane, and he said to them, "Sit here while I go over there and pray." ³⁷He took Peter and the two sons of Zebedee along with him, and he began to be sorrowful and troubled. ³⁸Then he said to them, "My soul is overwhelmed with sorrow to the point of death. Stay here and keep watch with me."

³⁹Going a little farther, he fell with his face to the ground and prayed, "My Father, if it is possible, may this cup be taken from me. Yet not as I will, but as you will."

⁴⁰Then he returned to his disciples and found them sleeping. "Could you men not keep watch with me for one hour?" he asked Peter. ⁴¹"Watch and pray so that you will not fall into temptation. The spirit is willing, but the body is weak."

⁴²He went away a second time and prayed, "My Father, if it is not possible for this cup to be taken away unless I drink it, may your will be done."

⁴³When he came back, he again found them sleeping, because their eyes were heavy. ⁴⁴So he left them and went away once more and prayed the third time, saying the same thing.

⁴⁵Then he returned to the disciples and said to them, "Are you still sleeping and resting? Look, the hour is near, and the Son of Man is betrayed into the hands of sinners. ⁴⁶Rise, let us go! Here comes my betrayer!" (Matthew 26:36-46)

Jesus left the city and quietly led the eleven toward His usual place of retreat on the slope of Olivet. Nothing was said along the way as Jesus had already spoken His last words of warning and encouragement, and a somber mood had fallen on the disciples. Although they sensed His sorrow and dread, they must not have realized how close He was to death because they all fell asleep while He was praying.

10. What aspect of Jesus' character sustained Him though this terrible agony?

In what area of your life do you feel particularly vulnerable to temptation?

11. What temptations were the disciples about to face? What help did Jesus offer them?

12. What can we learn from Jesus' example about submitting to God?

When can you spend some quality time in prayer this week so that you will not give in to temptation?

13. According to Jesus, what concrete action can we take to resist temptation?

JESUS IS BETRAYED AND ARRESTED
Matthew 26:47-56, Mark 14:43-52,
Luke 22:47-53, John 18:2-11

²Now Judas, who betrayed him, knew the place, because Jesus had often met there with his disciples. ³So Judas came to the grove, guiding a detachment of soldiers and some officials from the chief priests and Pharisees. They were carrying torches, lanterns and weapons.

⁴Jesus, knowing all that was going to happen to him, went out and asked them, "Who is it you want?"

⁵"Jesus of Nazareth," they replied.

"I am he," Jesus said. (And Judas the traitor was standing there with them.) ⁶When Jesus said, "I am he," they drew back and fell to the ground.

⁷Again he asked them, "Who is it you want?" And they said, "Jesus of Nazareth."

⁸"I told you that I am he," Jesus answered. "If you are looking for me, then let these men go." ⁹This happened so that the words he had spoken would be fulfilled: "I have not lost one of those you gave me."

¹⁰Then Simon Peter, who had a sword, drew it and struck the high priest's servant, cutting off his right ear. (The servant's name was Malchus.)

¹¹Jesus commanded Peter, "Put your sword away! Shall I not drink the cup the Father has given me?" (John 18:2-11)

Judas knew he hadn't fooled Jesus. He knew all the right things to say to convince everyone else, but Jesus saw the jealousy, fear, and greed in Judas's heart. Jesus' all-knowing stare intensified Judas's bitterness and anger. He agreed to officially identify and accuse Jesus and led a band of armed soldiers to apprehend Him. Just hours earlier, the disciples had vowed their allegiance to Jesus. But at this crucial moment, they all ran away!

> What do you want to remember the next time a friend or family member disappoints you?

14. Why do you think the religious leaders chose to arrest Jesus at night in a private place?

How can you prepare yourself to stand strong the next time your commitment to Christ is tested?

15. What do you think Jesus would want us to learn from His response to Judas and the religious leaders?

In what seemingly insignificant ways is your commitment to Jesus tested on a regular basis?

16. How do we typically respond when people let us down?

We would all like to think that if we were one of the disciples, we would have stood by Jesus. It's unlikely that we'll face intense persecution or suffering for Christ, but we are tested in a different way. The depth of our commitment to Christ is revealed in the choices we make every day. We prove our devotion by faithfully obeying Him and serving others for his glory.

> What can you do this week to remain faithful to Jesus, even in the small matters?

LESSON TWO
PRESUMED GUILTY

The injustice of Jesus' trial is appalling! The Jewish and Roman leaders, who were supposed to administer justice, knowingly sentenced an innocent man to die. We will study the examples of the religious leaders, judges, and disciples to see how they dealt with the guilt of betraying and condemning the Son of God. Their stories will reveal some important principles we can follow when dealing with guilt in our own life.

JESUS IS QUESTIONED AND CONDEMNED
Matthew 26:57,59-68; 27:1; Mark 14:53,55-65; 15:1; Luke 22:54,63-71; John 18:12-14,19-24

⁵⁷*Those who had arrested Jesus took him to Caiaphas, the high priest, where the teachers of the law and the elders had assembled. . . .*
⁵⁹*The chief priests and the whole Sanhedrin were looking for false evidence against Jesus so that they could put him to death.* ⁶⁰*But they did not find any, though many false witnesses came forward.*
Finally two came forward ⁶¹*and declared, "This fellow said, 'I am able to destroy the temple of God and rebuild it in three days.'"*

> *To this you were called, because Christ suffered for you, leaving you an example, that you should follow in his steps. "He committed no sin, and no deceit was found in his mouth." When they hurled their insults at him, he did not retaliate; when he suffered, he made no threats. Instead, he entrusted himself to him who judges justly.*
> (1 Peter 2:21-23)

⁶²*Then the high priest stood up and said to Jesus, "Are you not going to answer? What is this testimony that these men are bringing against you?" ⁶³But Jesus remained silent.*

The high priest said to him, "I charge you under oath by the living God: Tell us if you are the Christ, the Son of God."

⁶⁴*"Yes, it is as you say," Jesus replied. "But I say to all of you: In the future you will see the Son of Man sitting at the right hand of the Mighty One and coming on the clouds of heaven."*

⁶⁵*Then the high priest tore his clothes and said, "He has spoken blasphemy! Why do we need any more witnesses? Look, now you have heard the blasphemy. ⁶⁶What do you think?"*

"He is worthy of death," they answered.

⁶⁷*Then they spit in his face and struck him with their fists. Others slapped him ⁶⁸and said, "Prophesy to us, Christ. Who hit you?"*

¹*Early in the morning, all the chief priests and the elders of the people came to the decision to put Jesus to death.* (Matthew 26:57,59-68; 27:1)

In the middle of the night, a mob of religious leaders dragged Jesus from one hearing to the next, determined to have Him killed before the Sabbath. They were willing to do anything necessary to get rid of Him — they broke their own laws to expedite the process, they changed the charges against Him to please the different judges, they pressured false witnesses to lie under oath, and they never allowed Him a proper defense. The leaders obviously cared more about carrying out their plot than doing what was right.

1. How did Jesus respond to His unfair treatment?

2. Why didn't Jesus answer His accusers at His trial?

3. What do these trials reveal about the integrity of the Jewish leaders?

4. What do you observe about Jesus as a person from the way He behaved in this trial?

> What do you want to remember the next time someone mistreats you?

5. What can we learn from Jesus' example about dealing with unfair treatment?

••
PETER DENIES KNOWING JESUS
Matthew 26:58,69-75; Mark 14:54,66-72; Luke 22:54-62; John 18:15-18,25-27

⁵⁴*Peter followed him at a distance, right into the courtyard of the high priest. There he sat with the guards and warmed himself at the fire....*

⁶⁶*While Peter was below in the courtyard, one of the servant girls of the high priest came by.* ⁶⁷*When she saw Peter warming himself, she looked closely at him.*

"You also were with that Nazarene, Jesus," she said.

⁶⁸*But he denied it. "I don't know or understand what you're talking about," he said, and went out into the entryway.*

⁶⁹*When the servant girl saw him there, she said again to those standing around, "This fellow is one of them."* ⁷⁰*Again he denied it.*

After a little while, those standing near said to Peter, "Surely you are one of them, for you are a Galilean."

⁷¹*He began to call down curses on himself, and he swore to them, "I don't know this man you're talking about."*

⁷²*Immediately the rooster crowed the second time. Then Peter remembered the word Jesus had spoken to him: "Before the rooster crows twice you will disown me three times." And he broke down and wept.* (Mark 14:54,66-72)

In one short night, Peter changed from a bold defender at the time of Jesus' arrest to a cursing coward during the trial. When he saw the man he believed to be the Messiah being beaten and abused, Peter was confused. The first time someone recognized him as a follower of Christ, Peter tried to hide. The second time, he flatly denied it. The last time, he swore on his life that he never knew Jesus. When Peter came to his senses, realizing that he had failed his dearest friend, he wept bitterly.

6. What caused Peter to change over the course of this night?

7. How do you think Peter's character and faith were affected by his failure?

8. In what ways was Peter's denial of Jesus different than Judas's betrayal?

With whom would you like to be more honest about your commitment to Christ?

9. When are we tempted to downplay or even deny our faith in Jesus?

••
JUDAS KILLS HIMSELF
Matthew 27:3-10, Acts 1:18-19

³When Judas, who had betrayed him, saw that Jesus was condemned, he was seized with remorse and returned the thirty silver coins to the chief priests and the elders. ⁴"I have sinned," he said, "for I have betrayed innocent blood."

"What is that to us?" they replied. "That's your responsibility."

⁵So Judas threw the money into the temple and left. Then he went away and hanged himself.

⁶The chief priests picked up the coins and said, "It is against the law to put this into the treasury, since it is blood money." ⁷So they decided to use the

money to buy the potter's field as a burial place for foreigners. ⁸That is why it has been called the Field of Blood to this day. ⁹Then what was spoken by Jeremiah the prophet was fulfilled: "They took the thirty silver coins, the price set on him by the people of Israel, ¹⁰and they used them to buy the potter's field, as the Lord commanded me." (Matthew 27:3-10)

Judas may have turned Jesus over to the religious leaders to try to force Him to prove His power and establish His earthly kingdom. But when Jesus refused to defend Himself and was condemned by the Jewish council, Judas was remorseful and tried to return the money they had given him. Judas realized that he had betrayed an innocent man—his overwhelming sense of guilt led him to commit suicide.

10. How did Judas try to undo his crime? Why?

11. Judas killed himself while Peter became a bold witness for Jesus Christ. What made the difference in their reaction to failing Christ?

What do you want to remember the next time God convicts you of sin?

12. In what different ways do we try to deal with a guilty conscience?

How can you thank God today that He doesn't hold your sins against you, but forgives you fully and completely?

13. What can we learn from the examples of Peter and Judas about the proper way to deal with sin and guilt?

∙∙

JESUS STANDS TRIAL BEFORE PILATE AND HEROD Matthew 27:2,11-31; Mark 15:1-20; Luke 23:1-25; John 18:28–19:16

²⁸*Then the Jews led Jesus from Caiaphas to the palace of the Roman governor. By now it was early morning, and to avoid ceremonial uncleanness the Jews did not enter the palace; they wanted to be able to eat the Passover.* ²⁹*So Pilate came out to them and asked, "What charges are you bringing against this man?"*

³⁰"If he were not a criminal," they replied, "we would not have handed him over to you."

³¹Pilate said, "Take him yourselves and judge him by your own law."

"But we have no right to execute anyone," the Jews objected. ³²This happened so that the words Jesus had spoken indicating the kind of death he was going to die would be fulfilled.

³³Pilate then went back inside the palace, summoned Jesus and asked him, "Are you the king of the Jews?"

³⁴"Is that your own idea," Jesus asked, "or did others talk to you about me?"

³⁵"Am I a Jew?" Pilate replied. "It was your people and your chief priests who handed you over to me. What is it you have done?"

³⁶Jesus said, "My kingdom is not of this world. If it were, my servants would fight to prevent my arrest by the Jews. But now my kingdom is from another place."

³⁷"You are a king, then!" said Pilate.

Jesus answered, "You are right in saying I am a king. In fact, for this reason I was born, and for this I came into the world, to testify to the truth. Everyone on the side of truth listens to me."

³⁸"What is truth?" Pilate asked. With this he went out again to the Jews and said, "I find no basis for a charge against him. ³⁹But it is your custom for me to release to you one prisoner at the time of the Passover. Do you want me to release 'the king of the Jews'?"

⁴⁰They shouted back, "No, not him! Give us Barabbas!" Now Barabbas had taken part in a rebellion.

¹Then Pilate took Jesus and had him flogged. ²The soldiers twisted together a crown of thorns and put it on his head. They clothed him in a purple robe ³and went up to him again and again, saying, "Hail, king of the Jews!" And they struck him in the face.

⁴Once more Pilate came out and said to the Jews, "Look, I am bringing him out to you to let

you know that I find no basis for a charge against him." ⁵*When Jesus came out wearing the crown of thorns and the purple robe, Pilate said to them, "Here is the man!"*

⁶*As soon as the chief priests and their officials saw him, they shouted, "Crucify! Crucify!"*

But Pilate answered, "You take him and crucify him. As for me, I find no basis for a charge against him."

⁷*The Jews insisted, "We have a law, and according to that law he must die, because he claimed to be the Son of God."*

⁸*When Pilate heard this, he was even more afraid,* ⁹*and he went back inside the palace. "Where do you come from?" he asked Jesus, but Jesus gave him no answer.* ¹⁰*"Do you refuse to speak to me?" Pilate said. "Don't you realize I have power either to free you or to crucify you?"*

¹¹*Jesus answered, "You would have no power over me if it were not given to you from above. Therefore the one who handed me over to you is guilty of a greater sin."*

¹²*From then on, Pilate tried to set Jesus free, but the Jews kept shouting, "If you let this man go, you are no friend of Caesar. Anyone who claims to be a king opposes Caesar."*

¹³*When Pilate heard this, he brought Jesus out and sat down on the judge's seat at a place known as the Stone Pavement (which in Aramaic is Gabbatha).* ¹⁴*It was the day of Preparation of Passover Week, about the sixth hour.*

"Here is your king," Pilate said to the Jews.

¹⁵*But they shouted, "Take him away! Take him away! Crucify him!"*

"Shall I crucify your king?" Pilate asked.

"We have no king but Caesar," the chief priests answered.

¹⁶*Finally Pilate handed him over to them to be crucified.*

So the soldiers took charge of Jesus. (John 18:28–19:16)

Pilate knew in his heart that Jesus was innocent and did not deserve the death penalty. When he told the crowds he found no reason to charge Jesus, they increased the pressure, threatening to report him to Caesar. He feared that standing up for the truth could cost him his career and perhaps even his life. Pilate washed his hands in an attempt to remove his own sense of guilt for condemning an innocent man.

14. What are some examples of ways that we sometimes try to get out of doing what is right?

> In what ways do you feel pressured by peers, coworkers, friends, or family to compromise your standards?

15. In what circumstances is it difficult to stand up for the truth?

Which Christian friend could help you stay true to your convictions, despite pressure from others?

16. How can we learn to resist pressure from others?

In light of what you've learned in this lesson, what specific changes do you need to make in the way you deal with sin and guilt?

We've learned several principles about how to deal with sin and guilt in this lesson. The example of the religious leaders and Roman judges shows us the danger of making excuses for our sin or trying to pass the blame on to others. Judas's life demonstrates how unresolved guilt can destroy a person. Let's follow Peter's example by being sensitive to the convicting work of the Holy Spirit, quickly repenting of sin, and accepting God's forgiveness.

LESSON THREE
THE FINAL STEP

✣

Jesus now entered the final step of the mission on which He was sent. Although He endured sufferings throughout His lifetime on earth, He now faced the most horrible pain of all. The hatred of sinful men and the powers of hell would descend on Him in all their fury. As we study the crucifixion and resurrection, we'll learn the reason for these events and how they affect our lives today.

He himself bore our sins in his body on the tree, so that we might die to sins and live for righteousness; by his wounds you have been healed. (1 Peter 2:24)

JESUS IS CRUCIFIED
Matthew 27:31-56, Mark 15:20-41, Luke 23:26-49, John 19:16-37

²⁶As they led him away, they seized Simon from Cyrene, who was on his way in from the country, and put the cross on him and made him carry it behind Jesus. ²⁷A large number of people followed him, including women who mourned and wailed for him. ²⁸Jesus turned and said to them, "Daughters of Jerusalem, do not weep for me; weep for yourselves and for your children. ²⁹For the time will come when you will say, 'Blessed are the barren women, the wombs that never bore and the breasts that never nursed!' ³⁰Then

"'they will say to the mountains, "Fall on us!"
and to the hills, "Cover us!"'

³¹For if men do these things when the tree is green, what will happen when it is dry?"

³²Two other men, both criminals, were also led out with him to be executed. ³³When they came to the place called the Skull, there they crucified him, along with the criminals—one on his right, the other on his left. ³⁴Jesus said, "Father, forgive them, for they do not know what they are doing." And they divided up his clothes by casting lots.

³⁵The people stood watching, and the rulers even sneered at him. They said, "He saved others; let him save himself if he is the Christ of God, the Chosen One."

³⁶The soldiers also came up and mocked him. They offered him wine vinegar ³⁷and said, "If you are the king of the Jews, save yourself."

³⁸There was a written notice above him, which read: THIS IS THE KING OF THE JEWS.

³⁹One of the criminals who hung there hurled insults at him: "Aren't you the Christ? Save yourself and us!"

⁴⁰But the other criminal rebuked him. "Don't you fear God," he said, "since you are under the same sentence? ⁴¹We are punished justly, for we are getting what our deeds deserve. But this man has done nothing wrong."

⁴²Then he said, "Jesus, remember me when you come into your kingdom."

⁴³Jesus answered him, "I tell you the truth, today you will be with me in paradise."

⁴⁴It was now about the sixth hour, and darkness came over the whole land until the ninth hour, ⁴⁵for the sun stopped shining. And the curtain of the temple was torn in two. ⁴⁶Jesus called out with a loud voice, "Father, into your hands I commit my spirit." When he had said this, he breathed his last.

⁴⁷The centurion, seeing what had happened, praised God and said, "Surely this was a righteous man." ⁴⁸When all the people who had gathered to

witness this sight saw what took place, they beat their breasts and went away. ⁴⁹But all those who knew him, including the women who had followed him from Galilee, stood at a distance, watching these things. (Luke 23:26-49)

Crucifixion—the shame was unspeakable, the pain excruciating, and dying was slow and torturous. But God chose this for His own Son! Jesus died so that we could live. He suffered so we could be comforted. He was rejected so that we might be accepted. He separated Himself from the Father so we could enjoy eternity with Him. He bore our shame so that we could be free from guilt.

1. How did Jesus demonstrate His love for the people who crucified Him?

2. What did Christ's death accomplish?

How can you best express your gratitude to Jesus today for dying for your sins?

3. How do you feel when you think about the horrible abuse Jesus endured for your sin?

4. How would your life be different today if Jesus had saved Himself from the pain of the cross?

••
JESUS IS BURIED
Matthew 27:57-66, Mark 15:42-47, Luke 23:50-56, John 19:38-42

[38]Later, Joseph of Arimathea asked Pilate for the body of Jesus. Now Joseph was a disciple of Jesus, but secretly because he feared the Jews. With Pilate's permission, he came and took the body away. [39]He was accompanied by Nicodemus, the man who earlier had visited Jesus at night. Nicodemus brought a mixture of myrrh and aloes,

about seventy-five pounds. ⁴⁰Taking Jesus' body, the two of them wrapped it, with the spices, in strips of linen. This was in accordance with Jewish burial customs. ⁴¹At the place where Jesus was crucified, there was a garden, and in the garden a new tomb, in which no one had ever been laid. ⁴²Because it was the Jewish day of Preparation and since the tomb was nearby, they laid Jesus there. (John 19:38-42)

Joseph of Arimathea and Nicodemus, two wealthy and powerful religious leaders, had not participated in the plot to get rid of Jesus. They had been secret disciples, but now boldly asked Pilate for Jesus' body in order to give Him a proper burial. Jesus' death convinced them that He was the Son of God and they were finally willing to risk their reputations for Him. Jesus was willing to suffer and die for each one of us, the least we can do is openly admit our allegiance to Him.

5. What can we learn from the courageous example of these two men?

> How do you think Christ wants you to demonstrate your loyalty to Him this week?

6. Why are we sometimes embarrassed or nervous to tell others about our commitment to Christ?

What can you do if you feel scared to openly admit your Christian commitment?

7. In what ways do we try to hide our faith in Jesus?

8. What risks are involved in being a disciple of Christ today?

••
JESUS RISES FROM THE DEAD AND APPEARS TO THE WOMEN *Matthew 28:1-15, Mark 16:1-11, Luke 24:1-12, John 20:1-18*

¹*When the Sabbath was over, Mary Magdalene, Mary the mother of James, and Salome bought spices so that they might go to anoint Jesus' body.* ²*Very early on the first day of the week, just after sunrise, they were on their way to the tomb* ³*and they asked each other, "Who will roll the stone away from the entrance of the tomb?"*

⁴*But when they looked up, they saw that the stone, which was very large, had been rolled away.*

⁵As they entered the tomb, they saw a young man dressed in a white robe sitting on the right side, and they were alarmed.

⁶"Don't be alarmed," he said. "You are looking for Jesus the Nazarene, who was crucified. He has risen! He is not here. See the place where they laid him. ⁷But go, tell his disciples and Peter, 'He is going ahead of you into Galilee. There you will see him, just as he told you.'"

⁸Trembling and bewildered, the women went out and fled from the tomb. They said nothing to anyone, because they were afraid.

⁹When Jesus rose early on the first day of the week, he appeared first to Mary Magdalene, out of whom he had driven seven demons. ¹⁰She went and told those who had been with him and who were mourning and weeping. ¹¹When they heard that Jesus was alive and that she had seen him, they did not believe it. (Mark 16:1-11)

With the death and burial of Jesus, as far as His followers were concerned, it was all over. They were shocked and devastated by the recent events. Despite His repeated predictions, they had held fast to their hope that He would demonstrate His power to the world, save Israel from Roman oppression, and reign as their new King. They had no idea that Sunday morning would be the beginning of a new Kingdom, more glorious than they could ever imagine!

9. What proof do the Gospel writers give us that Jesus really did conquer death?

10. Why is Christ's resurrection pivotal for our faith in Him?

What steps will you take this week to better equip yourself to share the gospel with others?

11. What prevents people from believing that Jesus rose from the dead?

12. How would you respond to someone who contended that Jesus' resurrection was a hoax?

13. Why are we sometimes reluctant to tell others that Jesus rose from the dead?

> With whom could you share the good news of the gospel this week?

The angel who proclaimed the good news of Christ's resurrection told the women to go quickly and tell others. This is the most radical, life-changing news in history—Jesus rose from the dead just as He promised! Anyone who truly believes in Jesus' resurrection will want to share this great news with others.

LESSON FOUR
WE MEET AGAIN

The disciples thought their last memory of Jesus would be of Him hanging on the cross. His brutal death seemed to be a heavy and irretrievable disaster. They had believed He was the Messiah, but the crucifixion dispelled their hopes and dreams for the future. Nothing remained for them to do but return to their old homes and pick up where they had left off three years earlier. In this lesson, we'll see how they became fully convinced that Jesus had been raised from the dead. Their testimony will challenge us to decide what we believe about Jesus.

I know that my Redeemer lives, and that in the end he will stand upon the earth.
(Job 19:25)

JESUS APPEARS TO TWO BELIEVERS TRAVELING ON THE ROAD Mark 16:12-13, Luke 24:13-35

¹³*Now that same day two of them were going to a village called Emmaus, about seven miles from Jerusalem.* ¹⁴*They were talking with each other about everything that had happened.* ¹⁵*As they talked and discussed these things with each other, Jesus himself came up and walked along with them;* ¹⁶*but they were kept from recognizing him.*
¹⁷*He asked them, "What are you discussing together as you walk along?"*

They stood still, their faces downcast. ¹⁸One of them, named Cleopas, asked him, "Are you only a visitor to Jerusalem and do not know the things that have happened there in these days?"

¹⁹"What things?" he asked.

"About Jesus of Nazareth," they replied. "He was a prophet, powerful in word and deed before God and all the people. ²⁰The chief priests and our rulers handed him over to be sentenced to death, and they crucified him; ²¹but we had hoped that he was the one who was going to redeem Israel. And what is more, it is the third day since all this took place. ²²In addition, some of our women amazed us. They went to the tomb early this morning ²³but didn't find his body. They came and told us that they had seen a vision of angels, who said he was alive. ²⁴Then some of our companions went to the tomb and found it just as the women had said, but him they did not see."

²⁵He said to them, "How foolish you are, and how slow of heart to believe all that the prophets have spoken! ²⁶Did not the Christ have to suffer these things and then enter his glory?" ²⁷And beginning with Moses and all the Prophets, he explained to them what was said in all the Scriptures concerning himself.

²⁸As they approached the village to which they were going, Jesus acted as if he were going farther. ²⁹But they urged him strongly, "Stay with us, for it is nearly evening; the day is almost over." So he went in to stay with them.

³⁰When he was at the table with them, he took bread, gave thanks, broke it and began to give it to them. ³¹Then their eyes were opened and they recognized him, and he disappeared from their sight. ³²They asked each other, "Were not our hearts burning within us while he talked with us on the road and opened the Scriptures to us?"

³³They got up and returned at once to Jerusalem. There they found the Eleven and those with them, assembled together ³⁴and saying, "It is true! The Lord has risen and has appeared to

Simon." ³⁵Then the two told what had happened on the way, and how Jesus was recognized by them when he broke the bread. (Luke 24:13-35)

Cleopas and another person, two of Christ's followers, had probably remained in Jerusalem for the Feast of Unleavened Bread and were now on their way home to Emmaus. While they were walking slowly along the road and reminiscing mournfully over the momentous events of the past week, Jesus Himself joined them. They were so busy lamenting their loss and disappointment that they didn't even recognize Him!

1. Why did Jesus reveal Himself progressively to these disciples instead of simply telling them at the beginning who He was?

2. What did the two do as soon as they realized they had seen Jesus face to face?

3. How did Jesus reveal Himself to you over time before you recognized and received Him as your Lord?

What could you do to become more sensitive to the Holy Spirit's leading in your life?

4. Why are we sometimes slow to recognize God's working in our life?

• •
JESUS APPEARS TO THE DISCIPLES BEHIND LOCKED DOORS Mark 16:14, Luke 24:36-43, John 20:19-23

36While they were still talking about this, Jesus himself stood among them and said to them, "Peace be with you."
37They were startled and frightened, thinking they saw a ghost. 38He said to them, "Why are you troubled, and why do doubts rise in your minds? 39Look at my hands and my feet. It is I myself! Touch me and see; a ghost does not have flesh and bones, as you see I have."

⁴⁰*When he had said this, he showed them his hands and feet. ⁴¹And while they still did not believe it because of joy and amazement, he asked them, "Do you have anything here to eat?" ⁴²They gave him a piece of broiled fish, ⁴³and he took it and ate it in their presence.* (Luke 24:36-43)

After Jesus left the two disciples from Emmaus, they returned to Jerusalem and reported their experience to the apostles. As they were told of the Lord's appearance to Peter, suddenly Jesus appeared to the whole group. Through His words and actions, Jesus proved to them He wasn't a ghost or figment of their imagination. Just as He had promised, He had conquered death!

5. How did Jesus reassure and encourage the disciples?

6. What did Jesus do in front of His disciples to show them plainly that He had been physically resurrected?

> What do you need to do (or stop doing) to become a more effective witness for Christ?

7. What can we do to help others believe in the truth of the gospel?

8. What would you want to say or do if you met Jesus face to face? Why?

••
JESUS APPEARS TO THE DISCIPLES INCLUDING THOMAS John 20:24-31

²⁴*Now Thomas (called Didymus), one of the Twelve, was not with the disciples when Jesus came.* ²⁵*So the other disciples told him, "We have seen the Lord!"*

But he said to them, "Unless I see the nail marks in his hands and put my finger where the nails were, and put my hand into his side, I will not believe it."

²⁶*A week later his disciples were in the house again, and Thomas was with them. Though the*

doors were locked, Jesus came and stood among them and said, "Peace be with you!" ²⁷*Then he said to Thomas, "Put your finger here; see my hands. Reach out your hand and put it into my side. Stop doubting and believe."*

²⁸*Thomas said to him, "My Lord and my God!"*

²⁹*Then Jesus told him, "Because you have seen me, you have believed; blessed are those who have not seen and yet have believed."*

³⁰*Jesus did many other miraculous signs in the presence of his disciples, which are not recorded in this book.* ³¹*But these are written that you may believe that Jesus is the Christ, the Son of God, and that by believing you may have life in his name.* (John 20:24-31)

Although he is known as "Doubting Thomas," we can learn from Thomas's example. His doubt caused him to ask questions until he came to believe that Jesus had truly risen from the dead. His honesty about his doubts was better than the silent disbelief of many others. Stubbornly refusing to accept the truth harms our faith, but searching for answers to our questions can deepen our faith. When you experience doubts, actively seek answers from God's Word and mature believers.

9. How did Jesus deal with Thomas?

10. How does Jesus' response to Thomas encourage and challenge you?

What steps can you take this week to search for answers to a question you have about your faith?

11. What is the best way to deal with our spiritual questions and doubts?

••
JESUS APPEARS TO THE DISCIPLES WHILE FISHING *John 21:1-25*

¹Afterward Jesus appeared again to his disciples, by the Sea of Tiberias. It happened this way: ²Simon Peter, Thomas (called Didymus), Nathanael from Cana in Galilee, the sons of Zebedee, and two other disciples were together. ³"I'm going out to fish," Simon Peter told them, and they said, "We'll go with you." So they went out and got into the boat, but that night they caught nothing.

⁴*Early in the morning, Jesus stood on the shore, but the disciples did not realize that it was Jesus.*

⁵*He called out to them, "Friends, haven't you any fish?"*

"No," they answered.

⁶*He said, "Throw your net on the right side of the boat and you will find some." When they did, they were unable to haul the net in because of the large number of fish.*

⁷*Then the disciple whom Jesus loved said to Peter, "It is the Lord!" As soon as Simon Peter heard him say, "It is the Lord," he wrapped his outer garment around him (for he had taken it off) and jumped into the water.* ⁸*The other disciples followed in the boat, towing the net full of fish, for they were not far from shore, about a hundred yards.* ⁹*When they landed, they saw a fire of burning coals there with fish on it, and some bread.*

¹⁰*Jesus said to them, "Bring some of the fish you have just caught."*

¹¹*Simon Peter climbed aboard and dragged the net ashore. It was full of large fish, 153, but even with so many the net was not torn.* ¹²*Jesus said to them, "Come and have breakfast." None of the disciples dared ask him, "Who are you?" They knew it was the Lord.* ¹³*Jesus came, took the bread and gave it to them, and did the same with the fish.* ¹⁴*This was now the third time Jesus appeared to his disciples after he was raised from the dead.*

¹⁵*When they had finished eating, Jesus said to Simon Peter, "Simon son of John, do you truly love me more than these?"*

"Yes, Lord," he said, "you know that I love you."

Jesus said, "Feed my lambs."

¹⁶*Again Jesus said, "Simon son of John, do you truly love me?"*

He answered, "Yes, Lord, you know that I love you."

Jesus said, "Take care of my sheep."

¹⁷*The third time he said to him, "Simon son of John, do you love me?"*

Peter was hurt because Jesus asked him the third time, "Do you love me?" He said, "Lord, you know all things; you know that I love you."

Jesus said, "Feed my sheep. [18]I tell you the truth, when you were younger you dressed yourself and went where you wanted; but when you are old you will stretch out your hands, and someone else will dress you and lead you where you do not want to go." [19]Jesus said this to indicate the kind of death by which Peter would glorify God. Then he said to him, "Follow me!"

[20]Peter turned and saw that the disciple whom Jesus loved was following them. (This was the one who had leaned back against Jesus at the supper and had said, "Lord, who is going to betray you?") [21]When Peter saw him, he asked, "Lord, what about him?"

[22]Jesus answered, "If I want him to remain alive until I return, what is that to you? You must follow me." [23]Because of this, the rumor spread among the brothers that this disciple would not die. But Jesus did not say that he would not die; he only said, "If I want him to remain alive until I return, what is that to you?"

[24]This is the disciple who testifies to these things and who wrote them down. We know that his testimony is true.

[25]Jesus did many other things as well. If every one of them were written down, I suppose that even the whole world would not have room for the books that would be written. (John 21:1-25)

The previous week had been a stressful and confusing time for the disciples. They had returned to the familiarity of the Sea of Galilee for a break from the whirlwind activity of Jerusalem. While they were fishing, Jesus appeared again to seven of them. During this time, Jesus focused His attention on Peter, who felt devastated after denying Christ at his trial. Jesus lovingly took the time to reassure Peter and commission him for ministry.

12. Why did Jesus repeatedly question Peter's love for Him?

13. What did Jesus mean when He told Peter to "Feed my lambs"?

What act of service could you do this week to demonstrate your devotion to Christ?

14. In what ways does Jesus want us to serve other believers?

What has convinced you that Jesus is the Son of God?

What difference will your belief in Jesus make in your life this week?

After the horror of seeing Jesus crucified, the disciples experienced the immense joy of seeing Him alive again! We learn in this lesson that each one made up his own mind to believe in Christ's resurrection. Even though we don't have the privilege of seeing Jesus face to face, we have the testimony of those who did in the Bible. Jesus says that we are blessed if we believe without actually seeing Him.

LESSON FIVE
SPREAD THE WORD!

We've all started projects and then laid them aside before they were finished. Our excuses vary—some people get distracted by the appeal of bigger and better things, while others overestimate their time and abilities. A stack of unfinished projects may not have serious consequences. But Jesus has given us one task that we cannot leave unfinished—spreading the gospel message around the world. In this lesson, we'll discover how each of us can be involved in fulfilling the Great Commission.

He was given authority, glory and sovereign power; all peoples, nations and men of every language worshiped him. His dominion is an everlasting dominion that will not pass away, and his kingdom is one that will never be destroyed.
(Daniel 7:14)

JESUS GIVES THE GREAT COMMISSION
Matthew 28:16-20, Mark 16:15-18

¹⁶Then the eleven disciples went to Galilee, to the mountain where Jesus had told them to go. ¹⁷When they saw him, they worshiped him; but some doubted. ¹⁸Then Jesus came to them and said, "All authority in heaven and on earth has been given to me. ¹⁹Therefore go and make disciples of all nations, baptizing them in the name of the Father and of the Son and of the Holy Spirit, ²⁰and teaching them to obey everything I have commanded you. And surely I am with you always, to the very end of the age." (Matthew 28:16-20)

During the forty days Jesus spent with His disciples between His resurrection and ascension, He gave them specific instructions for their future. The mission on which Jesus sends *all* of His followers is to build disciples and develop disciple makers in every nation of the world. The task may seem impossible, but Jesus gives us all that we need to accomplish the job—spiritual gifts, the help and support of other believers, and most importantly, His presence in our heart.

How do you think Jesus wants you to be involved in fulfilling the Great Commission?

1. Why do we sometimes act as if the Great Commission (Matthew 28:18-20) is a suggestion rather than a command?

2. What are the various aspects involved in "making disciples"?

3. What typically hinders our witness for Christ?

> What special gifts has He given to equip you for the task?

4. In what ways have you experienced Jesus' presence in your life?

••••••••••••••••••••••••••••••••••••••
JESUS APPEARS TO THE DISCIPLES IN JERUSALEM Luke 24:44-49, Acts 1:3-8

⁴⁴He said to them, "This is what I told you while I was still with you: Everything must be fulfilled that is written about me in the Law of Moses, the Prophets and the Psalms."
⁴⁵Then he opened their minds so they could understand the Scriptures. ⁴⁶He told them, "This is what is written: The Christ will suffer and rise from the dead on the third day, ⁴⁷and repentance

and forgiveness of sins will be preached in his name to all nations, beginning at Jerusalem. ⁴⁸You are witnesses of these things. ⁴⁹I am going to send you what my Father has promised; but stay in the city until you have been clothed with power from on high." (Luke 24:44-49)

The forty-day period of instruction ended with Jesus' command to His disciples to remain in Jerusalem till the coming of the Holy Spirit. This time of waiting enabled the disciples to get a clearer understanding of Jesus and His mission. Now they understood more clearly what Jesus taught them before he died on the cross. They were ready to embark on a new life fulfilling Jesus' command to "make disciples of all nations."

5. What is the unique emphasis in each of the following statements of the Great Commission?

   Matthew 28:18-20

   Mark 16:15

   Luke 24:47

John 20:21

Acts 1:8

6. In light of these five statements of the Great Commission, how would you summarize the good news that Jesus wants us to take to the world?

7. What different responses have you received when sharing the good news with others?

What can you do now to better prepare yourself for any negative reactions you might receive while sharing the gospel?

8. What can we do when people refuse to accept the gospel message?

•••

JESUS ASCENDS INTO HEAVEN
Mark 16:19-20, Luke 24:50-53, Acts 1:9-12

¹⁹After the Lord Jesus had spoken to them, he was taken up into heaven and he sat at the right hand of God. ²⁰Then the disciples went out and preached everywhere, and the Lord worked with them and confirmed his word by the signs that accompanied it. (Mark 16:19-20)

As Jesus concluded His final charge and blessings to the disciples, He began rising into the air. Spellbound, the disciples watched as He disappeared into the clouds. Though Jesus' physical presence left earth, He sent His Holy Spirit to dwell in the hearts of all believers. The Holy Spirit empowers us to spread the gospel of salvation around the world.

9. How did the disciples react to what they had seen?

10. In what specific ways can we follow the example of the disciples?

How can you rely more on the Holy Spirit to help you share the good news with others?

11. What future event does Christ's ascension symbolize?

12. What does the ascension teach us about Christ's entire life on earth?

How can you best demonstrate your gratitude to Jesus for all that He has done for you?

What difference does Christ's resurrection and ascension make in your life today?

13. How would you summarize the importance of Christ's resurrection and ascension?

In what ways do you feel you personally know Christ better now than when you began this study?

The disciples were overjoyed to see Jesus again! After a brief time with Him, they began the enormous task of spreading the word of His resurrection. Jesus promises that we will all meet Him face to face. While we joyfully anticipate that day, He wants us to continue the important work the disciples began.

HARMONY OF THE LIFE AND MINISTRY OF JESUS CHRIST

	MATTHEW	MARK	LUKE	JOHN
	THE BEGINNING			
LESSON 1	The men who wrote the Gospels 1:1		1:1-4	
	God became a human being			1:1-18
	The ancestors of Jesus 1:1-17		3:23-38	
LESSON 2	An angel promises the birth of John to Zechariah		1:5-25	
	An angel promises the birth of Jesus to Mary		1:26-38	
	Mary visits Elizabeth		1:39-56	
	John the Baptist is born		1:57-80	
LESSON 3	An angel appears to Joseph 1:18-25			
	Jesus is born		2:1-20	
	Mary and Joseph bring Jesus to the temple		2:21-40	
	Visitors arrive from eastern lands 2:1-12			
	The escape to Egypt and return to Nazareth 2:13-23			
	Jesus' youth		2:41-52	
LESSON 4	John the Baptist prepares the way for Jesus 3:1-12	1:2-8	3:1-20	1:19-28
	John baptizes Jesus 3:13-17	1:9-11	3:21-22	1:29-34
	Satan tempts Jesus in the desert 4:1-11	1:12-13	4:1-13	
	The first disciples follow Jesus			1:35-51

	MATTHEW	MARK	LUKE	JOHN
LESSON 5	Jesus turns water into wine			2:1-11
	Jesus clears the temple			2:12-25
	Nicodemus visits Jesus at night			3:1-21
	John the Baptist tells more about Jesus			3:22-36
	CHALLENGING TRADITION			
LESSON 1	The Samaritan woman believes in Jesus			4:1-42
	Jesus preaches in Galilee 4:12	1:14-15	4:14-15	4:43-45
	Jesus heals a government official's son			4:46-54
	Jesus is rejected at Nazareth		4:16-30	
LESSON 2	Jesus moves to Capernaum 4:13-17		4:31	
	Four fisherman follow Jesus 4:18-22	1:16-20	5:1-11	
	Jesus heals and teaches people 4:23-25; 8:1-4,14-17; 9:1-8	1:21–2:12	4:33-44, 5:12-26	
	Jesus eats with sinners at Matthew's house 9:9-13	2:13-17	5:27-32	
LESSON 3	Religious leaders ask Jesus about fasting 9:14-17	2:18-22	5:33-39	
	Jesus heals people on the Sabbath 12:1-21	2:23–3:12	6:1-11	5:1-47
	Jesus selects the twelve disciples 10:2-4	3:13-19	6:12-16	
	Jesus gives the Beatitudes 5:1-16		6:17-26	
	Jesus teaches about the law 5:17-48		6:27-36	

	MATTHEW	MARK	LUKE	JOHN
LESSON 4	Jesus teaches about giving and prayer 6:1-8, 6:16–7:12		6:37-42	
	Jesus teaches about the way to Heaven 7:13-29		6:43-49	
	A Roman centurion demonstrates faith 8:5-13		7:1-10	
	Jesus raises a widow's son from the dead		7:11-17	
LESSON 5	Jesus eases John's doubt 11:1-30		7:18-35	
	A sinful woman anoints Jesus' feet		7:36–8:3	
	Religious leaders falsely accuse Jesus 12:22-45	3:20-30	11:14-28	
	Jesus describes His true family 12:46-50	3:31-35	8:19-21	

THE MESSIAH

	MATTHEW	MARK	LUKE	JOHN
LESSON 1	Jesus teaches through parables 13:1-52	4:1-34	8:4-18	
	Jesus calms the storm 8:23-27	4:35-41	8:22-25	
	Jesus sends the demons into a herd of pigs 8:28-34	5:1-20	8:26-39	
	Jesus heals people and raises a girl to life 9:18-34	5:21-43	8:40-56	
LESSON 2	The people of Nazareth refuse to believe 13:53-58	6:1-6		
	Jesus sends out the twelve disciples 9:35–10:42	6:7-13	9:1-6	
	Herod kills John the Baptist 14:1-12	6:14-29	9:7-9	
	Jesus feeds the five thousand 14:13-21	6:30-44	9:10-17	6:1-15

	MATTHEW	MARK	LUKE	JOHN
LESSON 3	*Jesus walks on water* 14:22-36	6:45-56		6:16-21
	Jesus is the true bread from Heaven			6:22-71
	Jesus teaches about inner purity 15:1-20	7:1-23		
	Jesus sends a demon out of a girl 15:21-28	7:24-30		
	Jesus feeds four thousand 15:29-39	7:31–8:10		
LESSON 4	*Religious leaders ask for a sign in the sky* 16:1-12	8:11-21		
	Jesus restores sight to a blind man	8:22-26		
	Peter says Jesus is the Messiah 16:13-20	8:27-30	9:18-20	
	Jesus predicts His death the first time 16:21-28	8:31–9:1	9:21-27	
LESSON 5	*Jesus is transfigured on the mountain* 17:1-13	9:2-13	9:28-36	
	Jesus heals a demon-possessed boy 17:14-21	9:14-29	9:37-43	
	Jesus predicts His death the second time 17:22-23	9:30-32	9:44-45	
	Peter finds the coin in the fish's mouth 17:24-27			
	FOLLOWING JESUS			
LESSON 1	*Jesus warns against temptation* 18:1-35	9:33-50	9:46-50	
	Jesus teaches about the cost of following Him 8:18-22, 19:1-2	10:1	9:51-62	7:2-9
	Jesus teaches openly at the temple			7:10-53
LESSON 2	*Jesus forgives an adulterous woman*			8:1-11
	Jesus teaches about Himself			8:12-59
	Jesus heals a blind man			9:1-41

	MATTHEW	MARK	LUKE	JOHN
LESSON 3	*Jesus is the good shepherd*			10:1-21
	Jesus sends out seventy-two messengers		10:1-24	
	Jesus tells the parable of the good Samaritan		10:25-37	
	Jesus visits Mary and Martha		10:38-42	
LESSON 4	*Jesus teaches His disciples about prayer* 6:9-15		11:1-13	
	Jesus exposes the religious leaders		11:37–12:12	
	Jesus warns the people		12:13–13:21	
	Religious leaders surround Jesus at the temple			10:22-42
LESSON 5	*Jesus heals and teaches people*		13:22–14:24	
	Jesus teaches about the cost of being a disciple		14:25-35	
	Jesus tells three parables		15:1-32	

ANSWERING THE CALL

	MATTHEW	MARK	LUKE	JOHN
LESSON 1	*Jesus teaches His disciples*		16:1–17:10	
	Jesus raises Lazarus from the dead			11:1-44
	Jesus heals ten men with leprosy		17:11-19	
LESSON 2	*Jesus teaches about the Kingdom of God*		17:20-37	
	Jesus tells two parables on prayer		18:1-14	
	Jesus teaches about marriage and divorce 19:3-12	10:2-12		
	Jesus blesses little children 19:13-15	10:13-16	18:15-17	

	MATTHEW	MARK	LUKE	JOHN
LESSON 3	*Jesus speaks to the rich young man* 19:16–20:16	10:17-31	18:18-30	
	Jesus teaches about serving others 20:17-28	10:32-45	18:31-34	
	Jesus heals a blind beggar 20:29-34	10:46-52	18:35-43	
LESSON 4	*Jesus brings salvation to Zacchaeus's home*		19:1-10	
	Jesus tells the parable of the king's ten servants		19:11-27	
	Religious leaders plot to kill Jesus			11:45-57, 12:9-11
	Jesus rides into Jerusalem on a donkey 21:1-11,14-17	11:1-11	19:28-44	12:12-13
LESSON 5	*Jesus curses the fig tree* 21:18-19	11:12-14		
	Jesus clears the temple again 21:12-13	11:15-19	19:45-48	
	Jesus summarizes His purpose and message			12:20-50
	Jesus says His disciples can pray for anything 21:20-22	11:20-25		

FINAL TEACHINGS

	MATTHEW	MARK	LUKE	JOHN
LESSON 1	*Religious leaders challenge Jesus' authority* 21:23-27	11:27-33	20:1-8	
	Jesus tells three parables 21:28–22:14	12:1-12	20:9-19	
	Religious leaders ask Jesus three questions 22:15-40	12:13-34	20:20-40	
	Religious leaders cannot answer Jesus' question 22:41-46	12:35-37	20:41-44	
LESSON 2	*Jesus warns against the religious leaders* 23:1-12	12:38-40	20:45-47	
	Jesus condemns the religious leaders 23:13-39			
	A poor widow gives all she has	12:41-44	21:1-4	
	Jesus tells about the future 24:1-51	13:1-37	21:5-38	

	MATTHEW	MARK	LUKE	JOHN
LESSON 3	Jesus tells about the final judgment 25:1-46			
	Religious leaders plot to kill Jesus 26:1-5	14:1-2	22:1-2	
	A woman anoints Jesus with perfume 26:6-13	14:3-9		12:1-8
	Judas agrees to betray Jesus 26:14-16	14:10-11	22:3-6	
LESSON 4	Disciples prepare for the Passover 26:17-19	14:12-16	22:7-13	
	Jesus washes His disciples' feet			13:1-20
	Jesus foretells His betrayal and suffering 26:20-25	14:17-21	22:14-16,21-30	13:21-30
LESSON 5	Jesus and His disciples have the Last Supper 26:26-28	14:22-24	22:17-20	
	Jesus talks with His disciples about the future 26:29-30	14:25-26		13:31–14:31
	Jesus predicts Peter's denial 26:31-35	14:27-31	22:31-38	
	Jesus teaches about the vine and the branches			15:1–16:4

THE CROSS AND THE RESURRECTION

	MATTHEW	MARK	LUKE	JOHN
LESSON 1	Jesus teaches about the Holy Spirit and prayer			16:5-33
	Jesus prays for Himself and believers			17:1-26
	Jesus agonizes in the garden 26:36-46	14:32-42	22:39-46	18:1
	Jesus is betrayed and arrested 26:47-56	14:43-52	22:47-53	18:2-11
LESSON 2	Jesus is questioned and condemned 26:57,59-68, 27:1	14:53,55-65, 15:1	22:54,63-71	18:12-14,19-24
	Peter denies knowing Jesus 26:58,69-75	14:54,66-72	22:54-62	18:15-18,25-27
	Judas kills himself (see also Acts 1:18-19) 27:3-10			
	Jesus stands trial before Pilate and Herod 27:2,11-31	15:1-20	23:1-25	18:28–19:16

	MATTHEW	MARK	LUKE	JOHN
LESSON 3	*Jesus is crucified* 27:31-56	15:20-41	23:26-49	19:16-37
	Jesus is buried 27:57-66	15:42-47	23:50-56	19:38-42
	Jesus rises from the dead and appears to the women 28:1-15	16:1-11	24:1-12	20:1-18
LESSON 4	*Jesus appears to two believers traveling on the road* 	16:12-13	24:13-35	
	Jesus appears to the disciples behind locked doors 	16:14	24:36-43	20:19-23
	Jesus appears to the disciples, including Thomas			20:24-31
	Jesus appears to the disciples while fishing			21:1-25
LESSON 5	*Jesus gives the Great Commission* 28:16-20	16:15-18		
	Jesus appears to the disciples in Jerusalem (see also Acts 1:3-8) 		24:44-49	
	Jesus ascends into Heaven (see also Acts 1:9-12) 	16:19-20	24:50-53	

www.ingramcontent.com/pod-product-compliance
Lightning Source LLC
Chambersburg PA
CBHW071841290426
44109CB00017B/1893